From

The Women's Press Ltd
124 Shoreditch High Street, London E1

pressing on —

Paula Youens is a British cartoonist whose work has been published in a number of publications including the *Observer, She, Honey* and *Cosmopolitan*. She has also shown her work in solo shows at The Workshop, London's only cartoonists' gallery.

Lone Thoughts from a Broad is the first published collection of Paula Youens' work.

PAULA YOUENS

Cartoons

Lone Thoughts from a Broad

The Women's Press

First published by The Women's Press Limited 1981
A member of the Namara Group
124 Shoreditch High Street, London E1 6JE

'The Great Myth' first reproduced in *Honey*, 1980
'Knitter II' first reproduced in the *Observer*, 1981

The Women's Press is a feminist publishing house. We aim
to publish lively, original works by women. A complete list
of our publications is available from us at the above address.

Lone Thoughts from a Broad has been
designed by Suzanne Perkins and
printed and bound in Great Britain by
Lowe & Brydone Limited, Leeds.

British Library Cataloguing in Publication Data

Youens, Paula
    Lone thoughts from a broad.
    1. English wit and humor, Pictorial
    2. Women – Caricatures and cartoons
    I. Title
    741.5'942   NC1479

ISBN 0-7043-3881-5

PAULA YOUENS

·HOW TO SHAPE YOUR PERSONALITY·

Perambulations I

NOT
allowed to be:-
Emotional
Upset
sensitive

Perambulations II

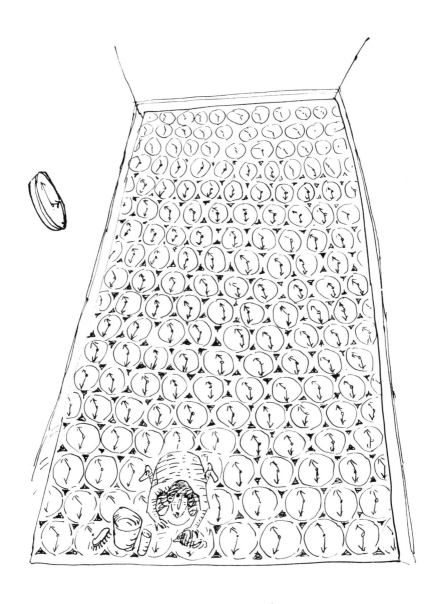

it's no good
shouting
about
things
dear

IT'S THE
GREAT MYTH..

Family T.V.

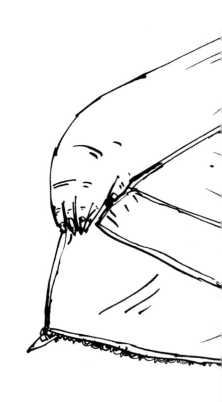

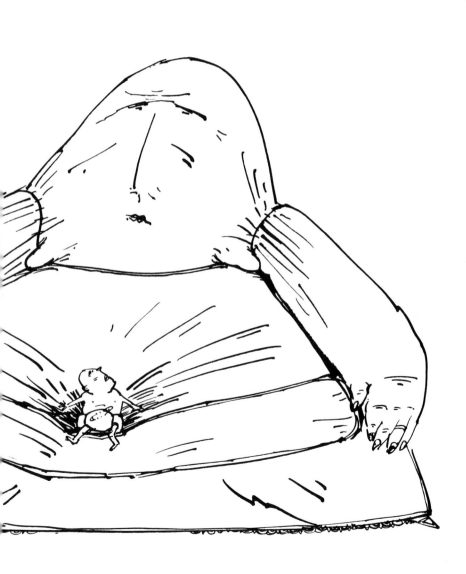

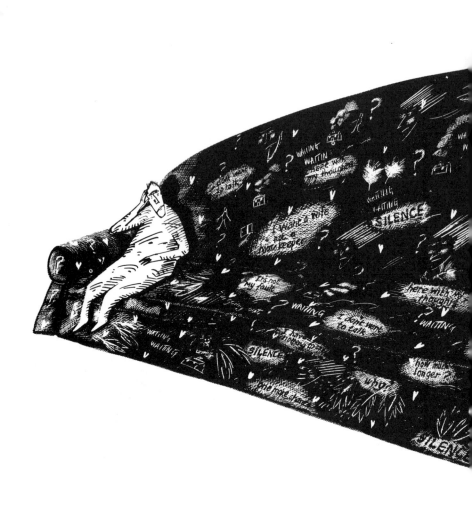

New meanings to old words

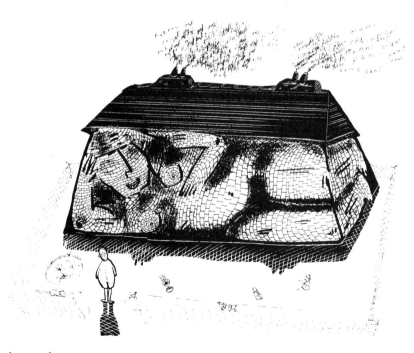

Hot house

Housebound

Housing shark

New meanings to old words: Housewife

New meanings to old words: Housewife

MRS. ATLAS

Mrs. Atlas

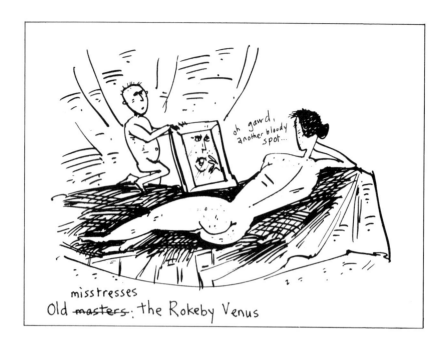

Old ~~masters~~: the Rokeby Venus

Old ~~masters~~ misstresses : Whistler's mother

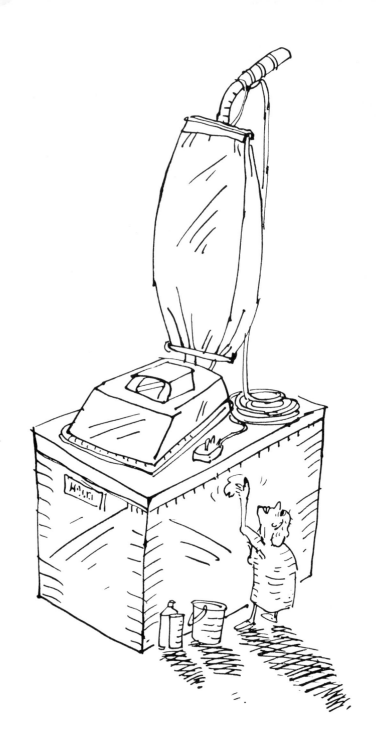

old people make
me worry about
death ...

with all these
worries
I can't find
the time
to be depressed ...

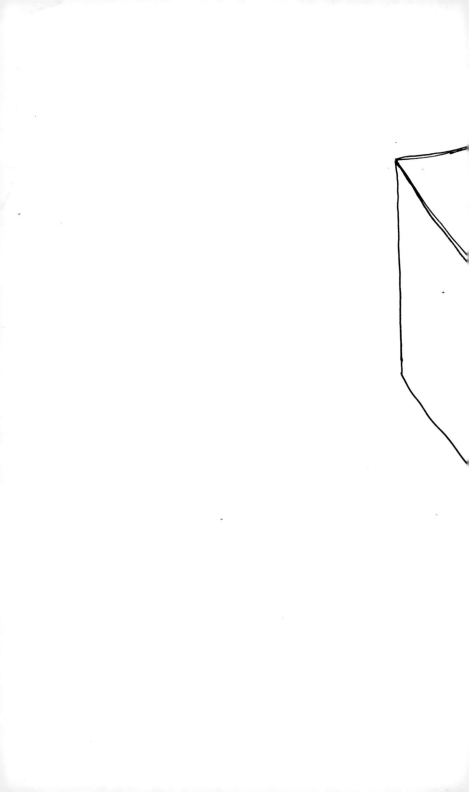

There's plenty of fish in the sea

Body shop

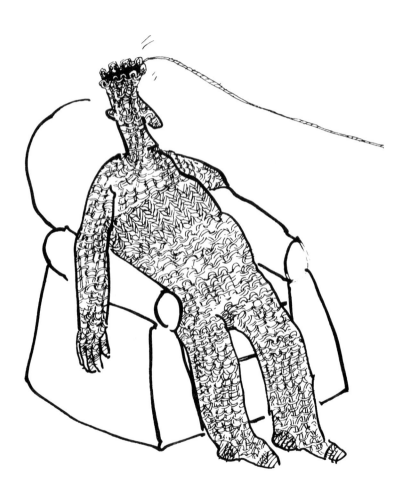

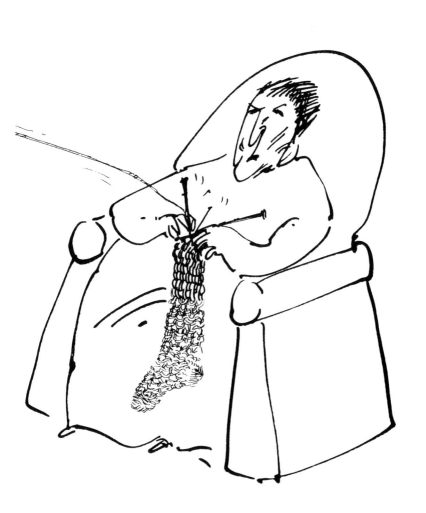

The art of family conversation